spot

HOLIDAYS

KWANZAA

by Mari Schuh

AMICUS | AMICUS INK

candles

corn

Look for these words and pictures as you read.

cup

feast

The room is decorated.
It is set for Kwanzaa!

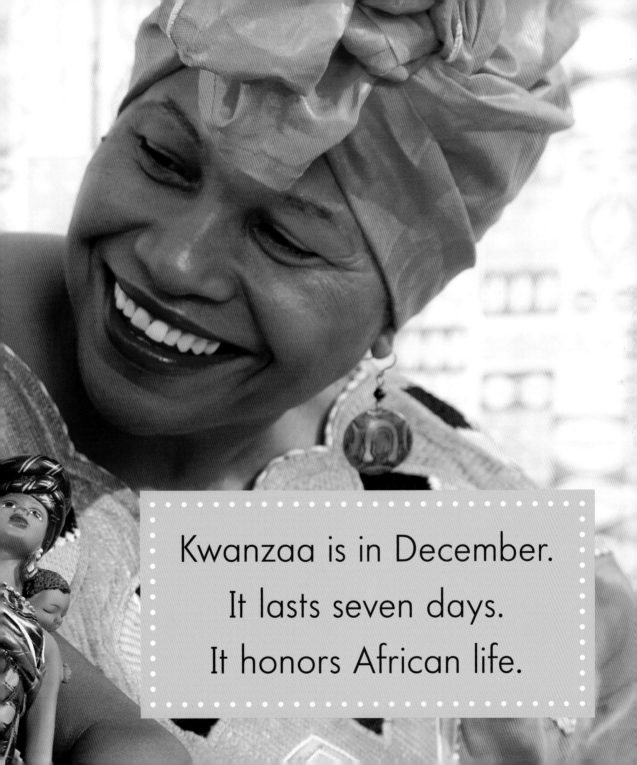

Kwanzaa is in December.
It lasts seven days.
It honors African life.

See the candles? There are seven.
One is lit each day.

candles

See the ears of corn?
They go on the table.
There is one for each child.

corn

cup

See the cup? It is the unity cup.
Everyone sips from it.

See the big feast?
It is called the karamu.
It is usually on the
sixth day.

feast

People play music.
They dance and
give thanks.

See the candles? There are seven.
One is lit each day.

candles

See the ears of corn?
They go on the table.
There is one for each child.

corn

candles

corn

Did you find?

cup

feast

See the cup? It is the unity cup.
Everyone sips from it.

cup

See the big feast?
It is called the karamu.
It is usually on the
sixth day.

feast

Spot is published by Amicus and Amicus Ink
P.O. Box 1329, Mankato, MN 56002
www.amicuspublishing.us

Library of Congress Cataloging-in-Publication Data
Names: Schuh, Mari C., 1975- author.
Title: Kwanzaa / by Mari Schuh.
Description: Mankato, Minnesota : Amicus/Amicus Ink,
  [2020] | Series: Spot holidays | Audience: K to Grade 3.
Identifiers: LCCN 2018048671 (print) | LCCN 2018050733
  (ebook) | ISBN 9781681518459 (pdf) | ISBN
  9781681518053 (library binding) | ISBN 9781681525334
  (paperback)
Subjects: LCSH: Kwanzaa—Juvenile literature. | African
  Americans—Social life and customs—Juvenile literature.
Classification: LCC GT4403 (ebook) | LCC GT4403 .S39
  2020 (print) | DDC 394.2612—dc23
LC record available at https://lccn.loc.gov/2018048671

Printed in China

HC 10 9 8 7 6 5 4 3 2 1
PB 10 9 8 7 6 5 4 3 2 1

Alissa Thielges, editor
Deb Miner, series designer
Veronica Scott, book designer
Holly Young and Shane Freed,
  photo researchers

Getty/Hill Street Studios cover, 16;
Shutterstock/Timothy R. Nichols 1;
iStock/AvailableLight 3; Getty/Rolf
Bruderer 4–5; Getty/Inti St. Clair 6–7;
Shutterstock/Luis Carlos Jimenez del
rio 8–9; Getty/Guy Cali 10–11; Getty/
Granger Wootz 12–13; Shutterstock/
santypan 14–15

KWANZAA